Trace Letters: Presch Handwriting Workbook

MW01154854

ISBN-13: 978-1548608439

ISBN-10: 1548608432

This Book
Belongs To

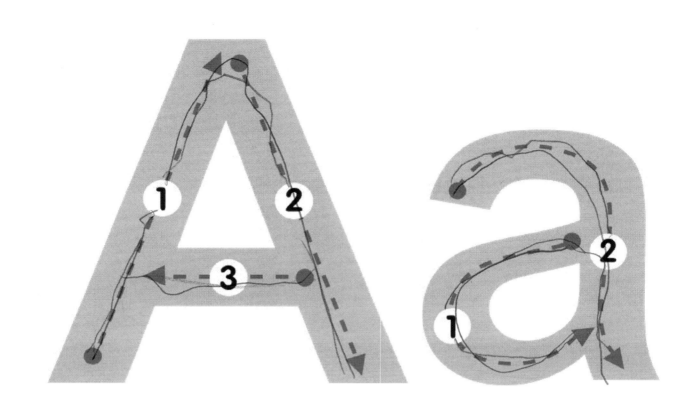

A is for ant

Aa Aa Aa Aa Aa Aa Aa

Aa Aa Aa Aa Aa Aa Aa

Aa Aa Aa Aa Aa Aa

Aa Aa Aa Aa Aa Aa

Aa Aa Aa Aa Aa Aa

Aa Aa Aa Aa Aa Aa

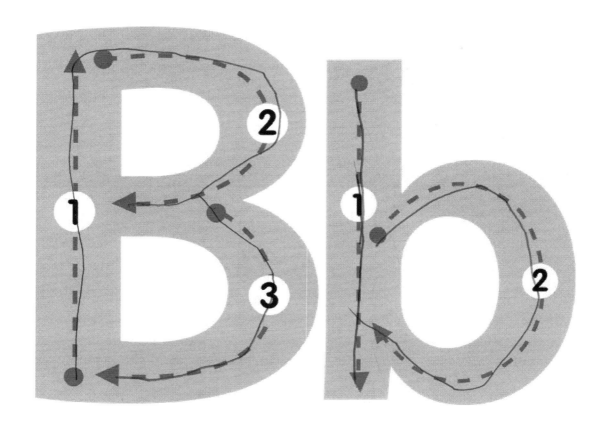

B is for butterfly

Bb Bb Bb Bb Bb Bb

Bb Bb Bb Bb Bb Bb

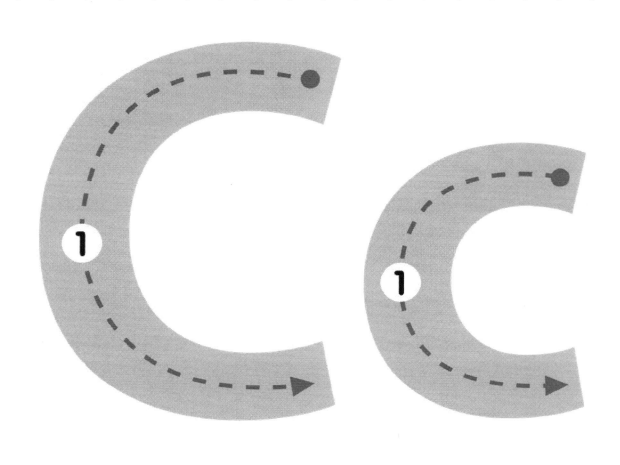

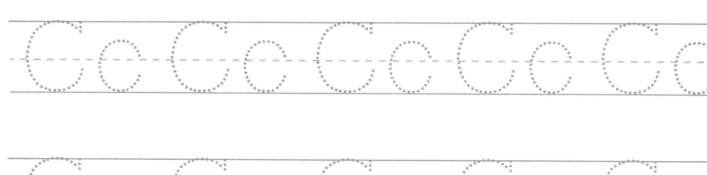

C is for canary

CcCcCcCcCcCcCc

CcCcCcCcCcCcCc

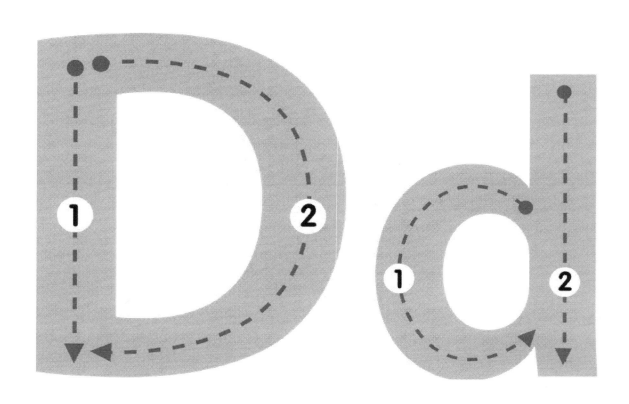

D is for dolphin

DdDdDdDdDdDd

DdDdDdDdDdDd

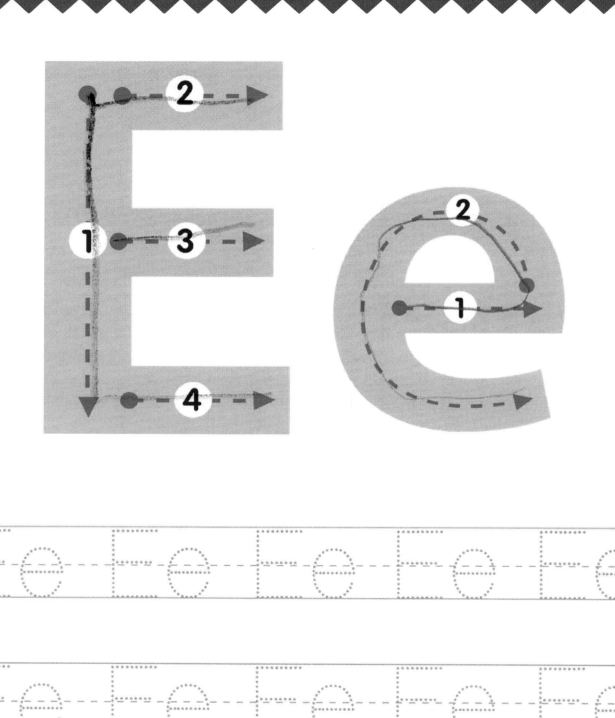

E is for eagle

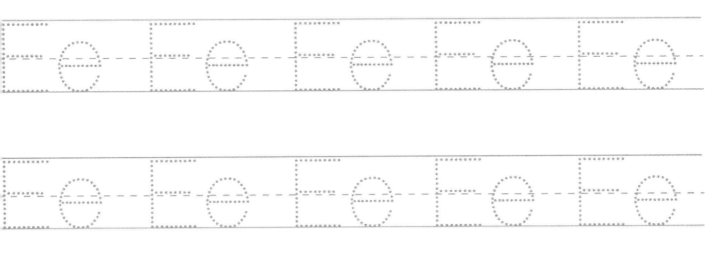

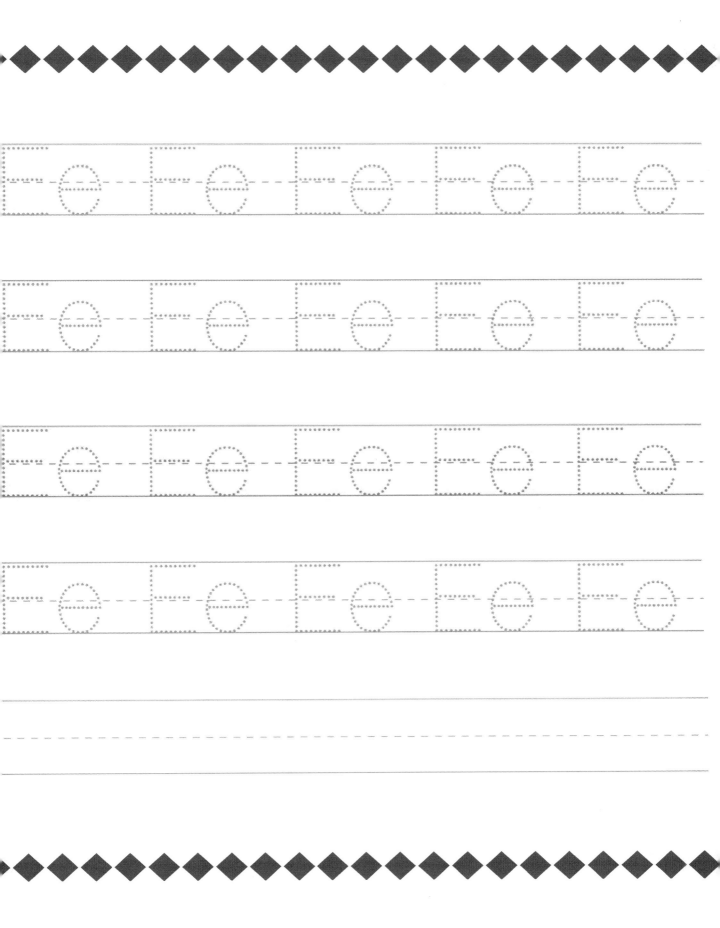

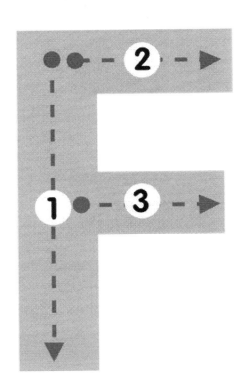
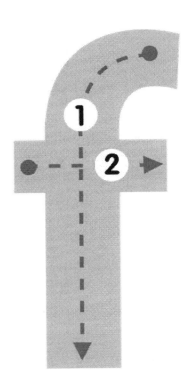

F is for flamingo

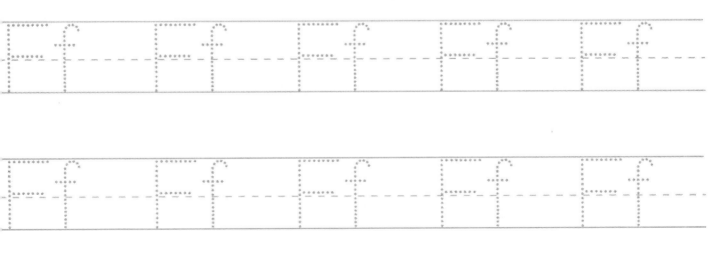

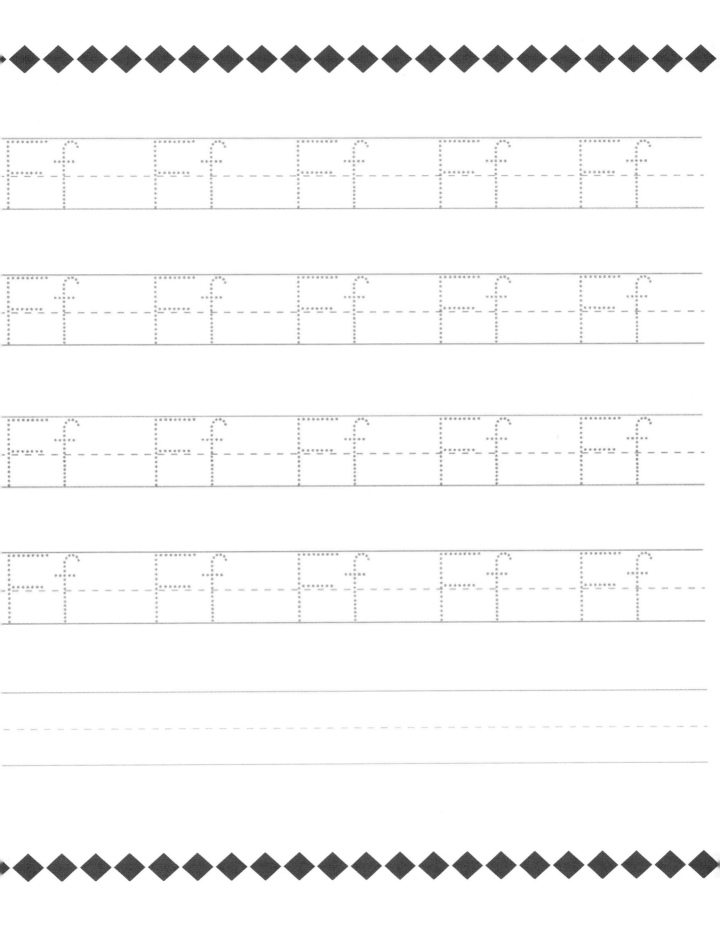

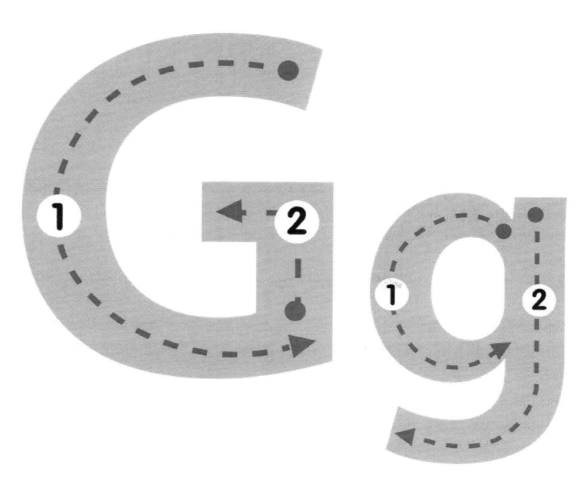

G is for grasshopper

GgGgGgGgGgGgGg

GgGgGgGgGgGgGg

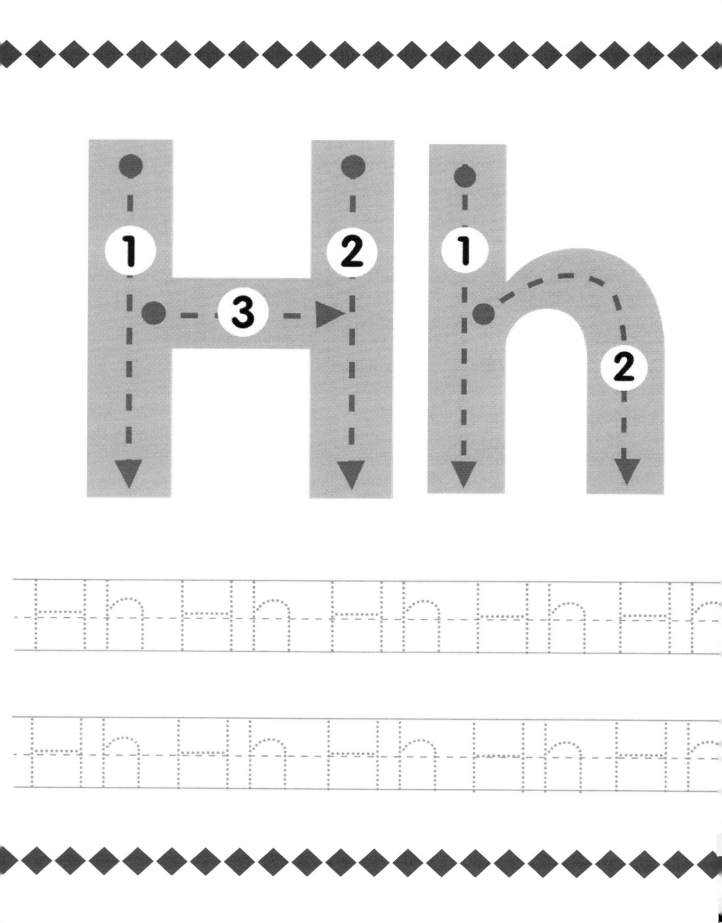

H is for hippopotamus

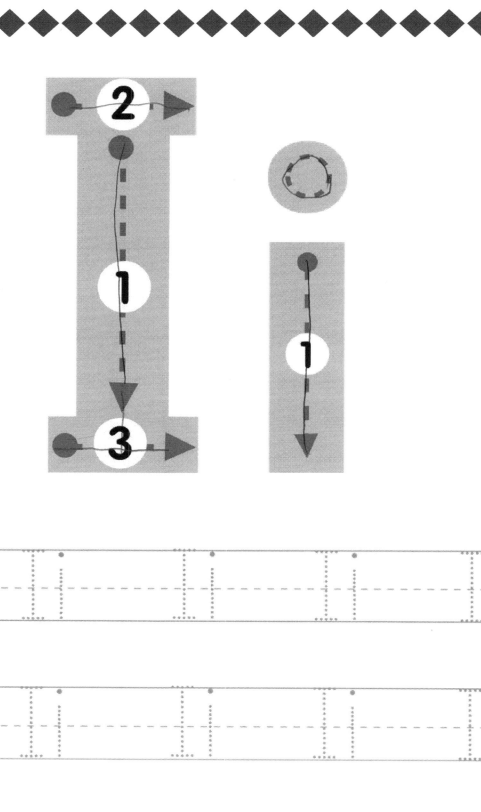

I is for iguana

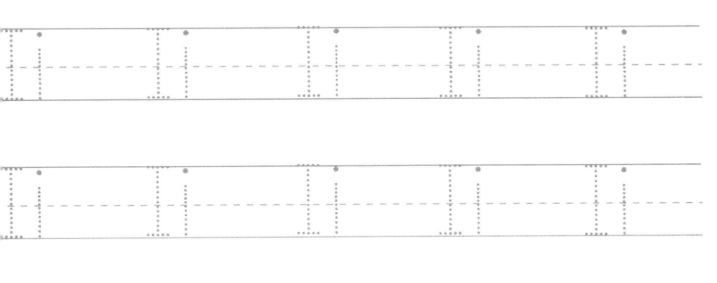

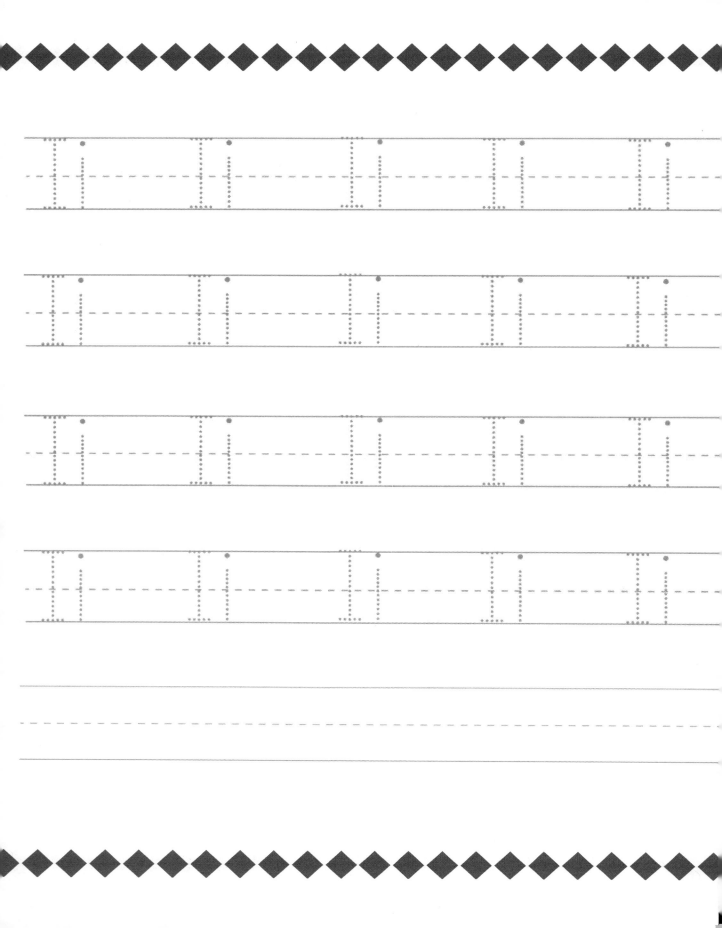

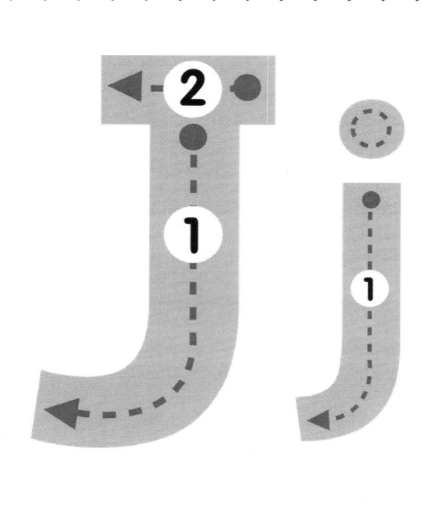

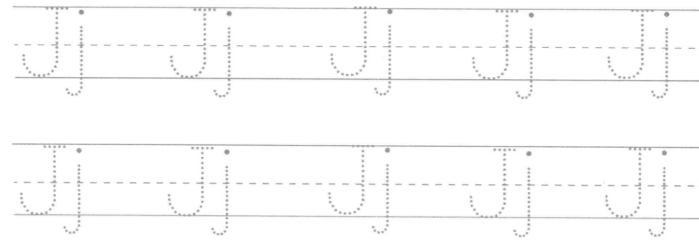

J is for jaguar

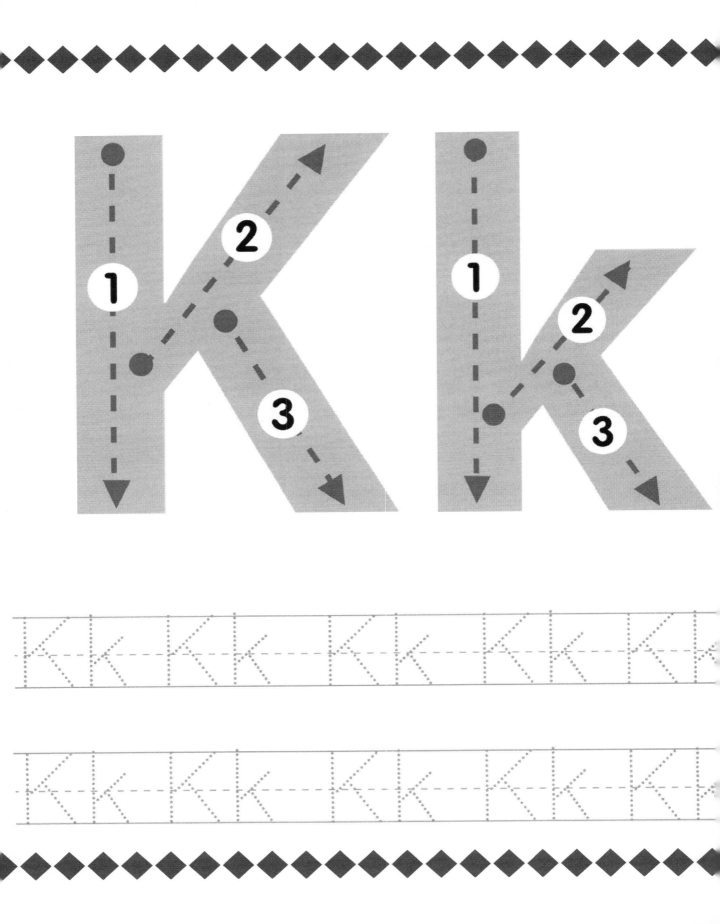

K is for kangaroo

Kk Kk Kk Kk Kk Kk Kk

Kk Kk Kk Kk Kk Kk Kk

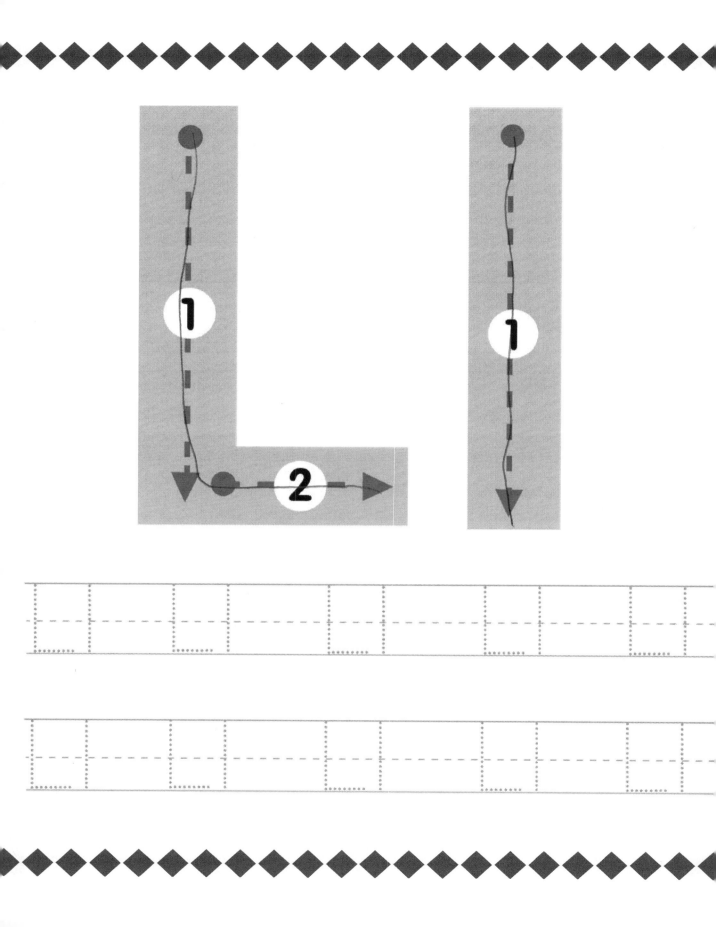

L is for lobster

M is for moose

Mm-Mm-Mm-Mm-Mm

Mm-Mm-Mm-Mm-Mm

Mm Mm Mm Mm Mm

Mm Mm Mm Mm Mm

Mm Mm Mm Mm Mm

Mm Mm Mm Mm Mm

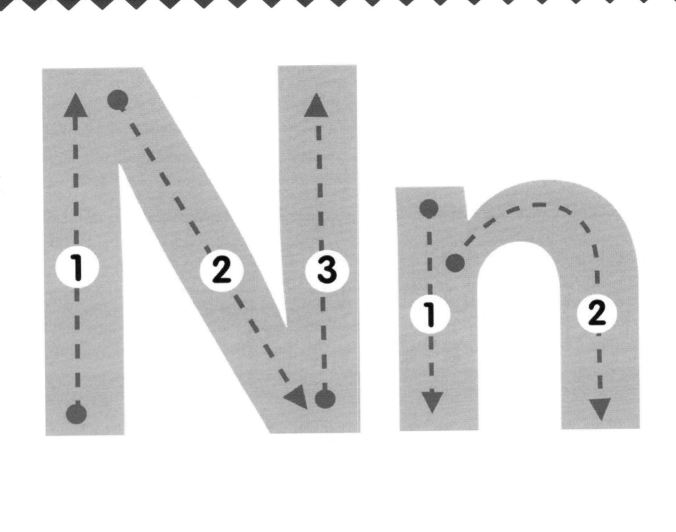

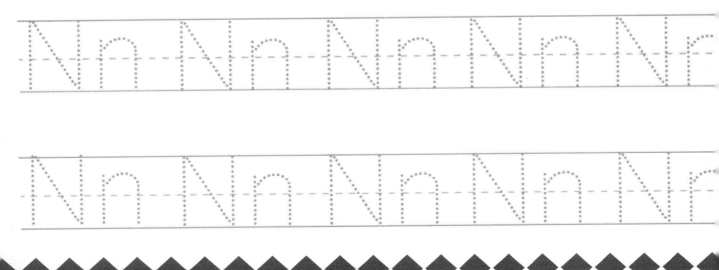

N is for narwhal

Nn Nn Nn Nn Nn Nn

Nn Nn Nn Nn Nn Nn

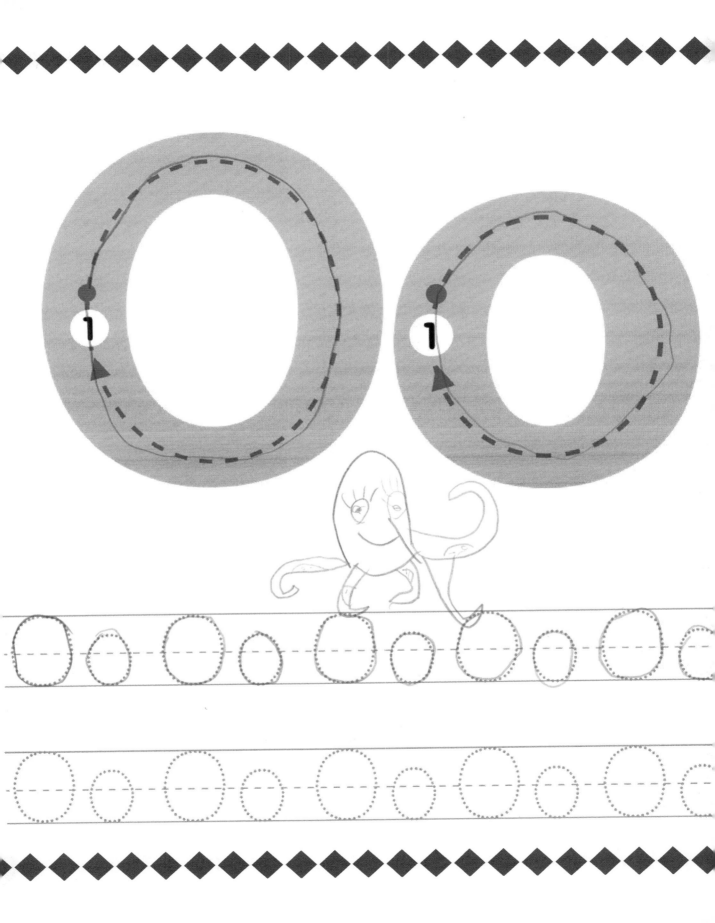

O is for octopus

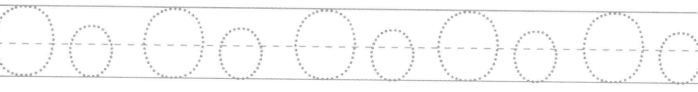

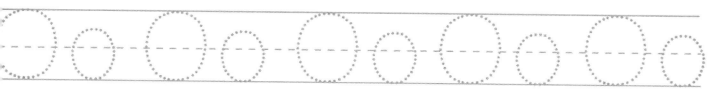

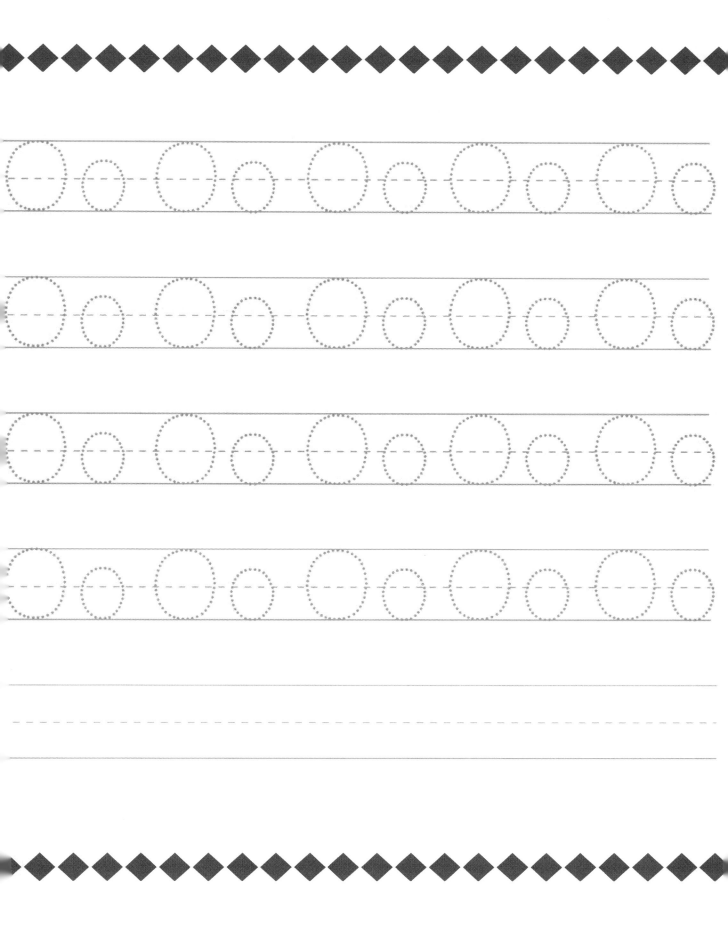

P is for penguin

Pp Pp Pp Pp Pp

Pp Pp Pp Pp Pp

Pp Pp Pp Pp Pp

Pp Pp Pp Pp Pp

Pp Pp Pp Pp Pp

Pp Pp Pp Pp Pp

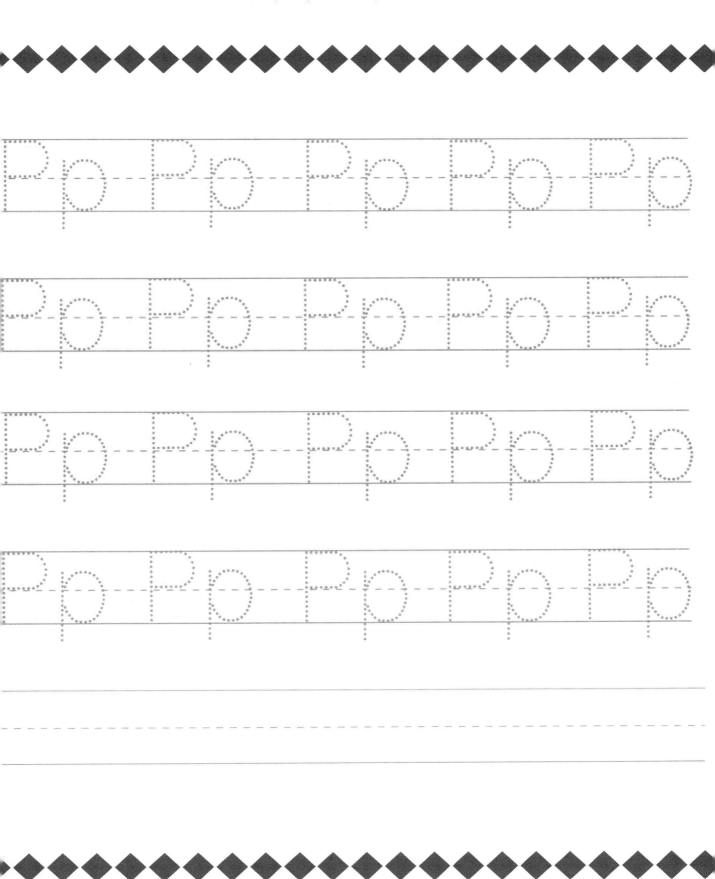

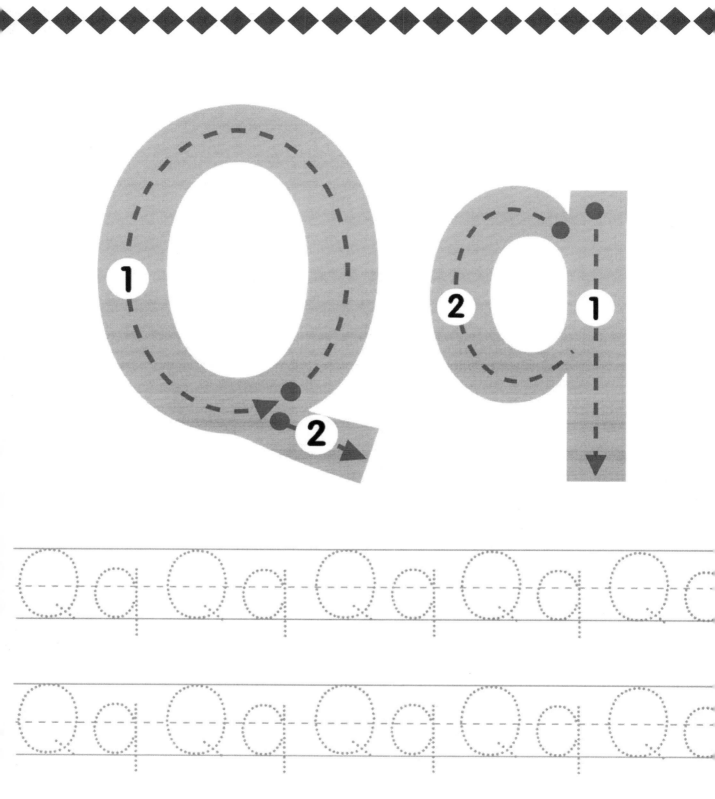

Q is for quail

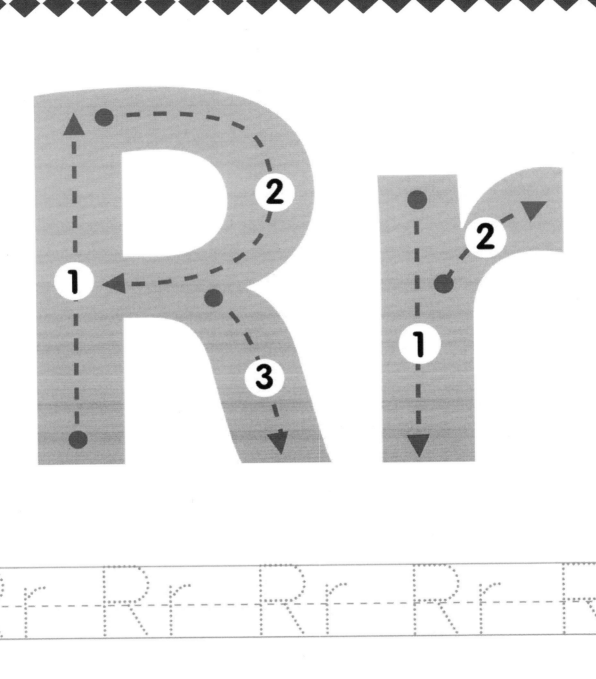

R is for rooster

Rr Rr Rr Rr Rr

Rr Rr Rr Rr Rr

S is for sloth

Ss Ss Ss Ss Ss Ss

Ss Ss Ss Ss Ss

Ss Ss Ss Ss Ss Ss

Ss Ss Ss Ss Ss

Ss Ss Ss Ss Ss

Ss Ss Ss Ss Ss

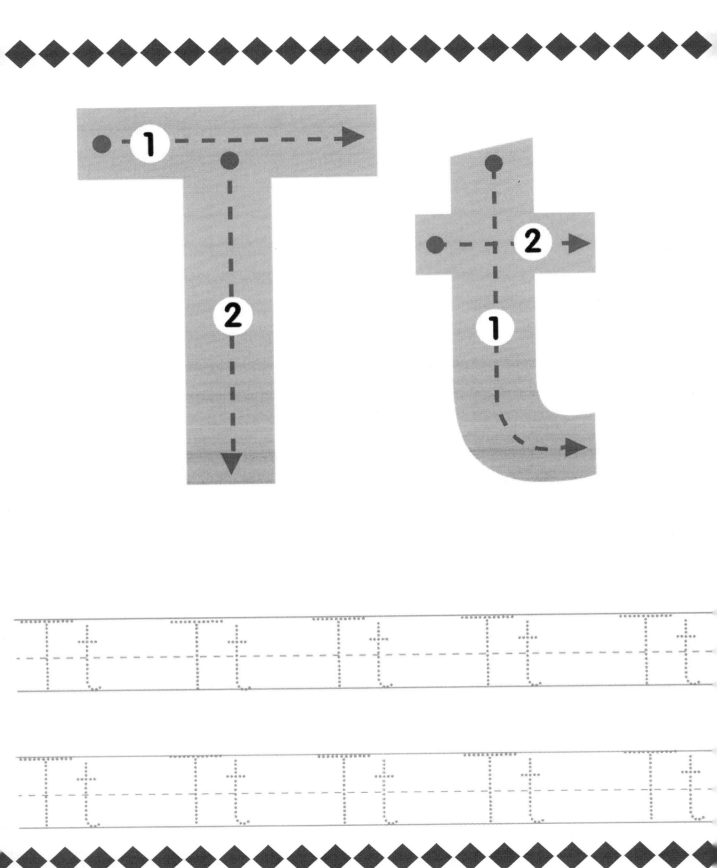

T is for toucan

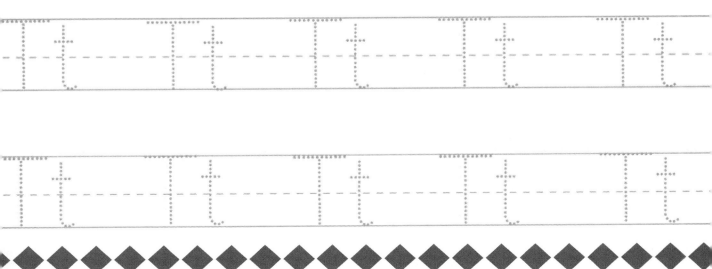

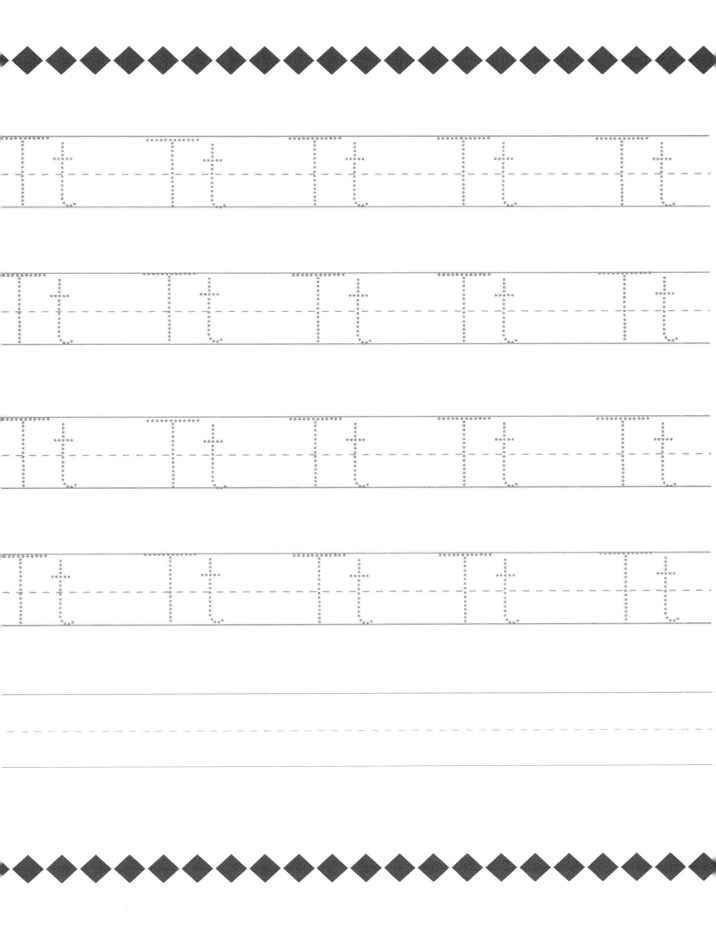

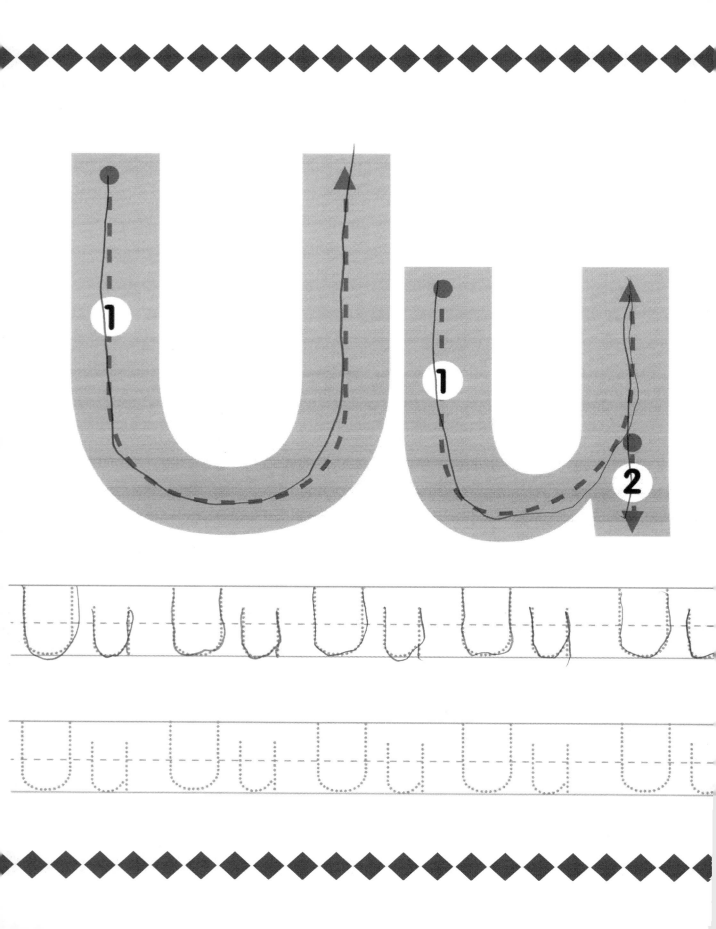

U is for unicorn

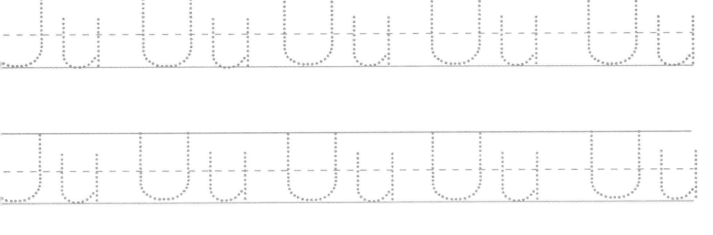

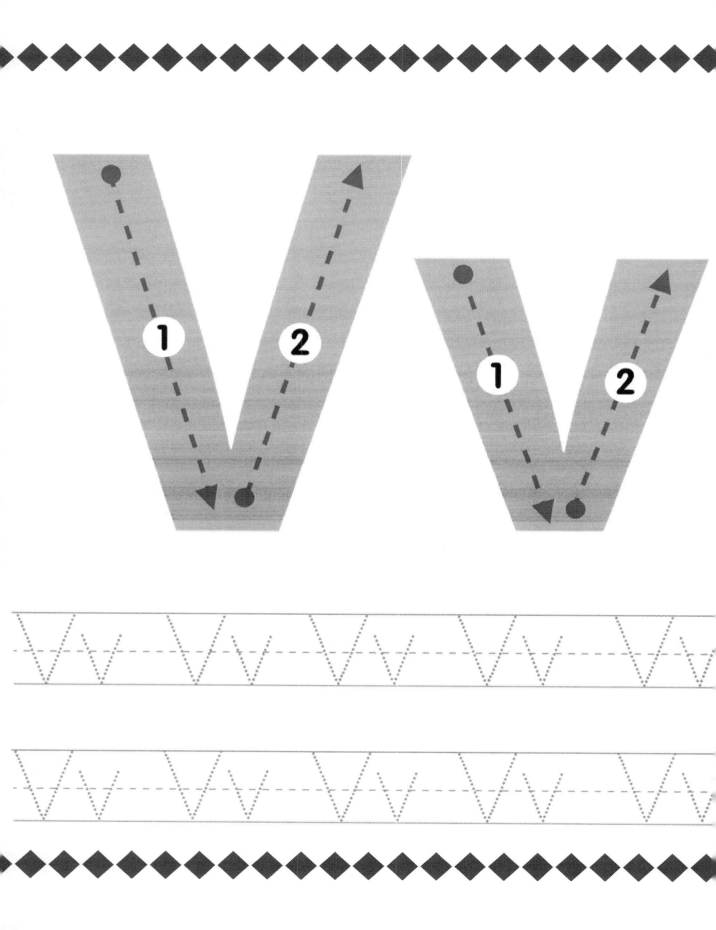

V is for vampire bat

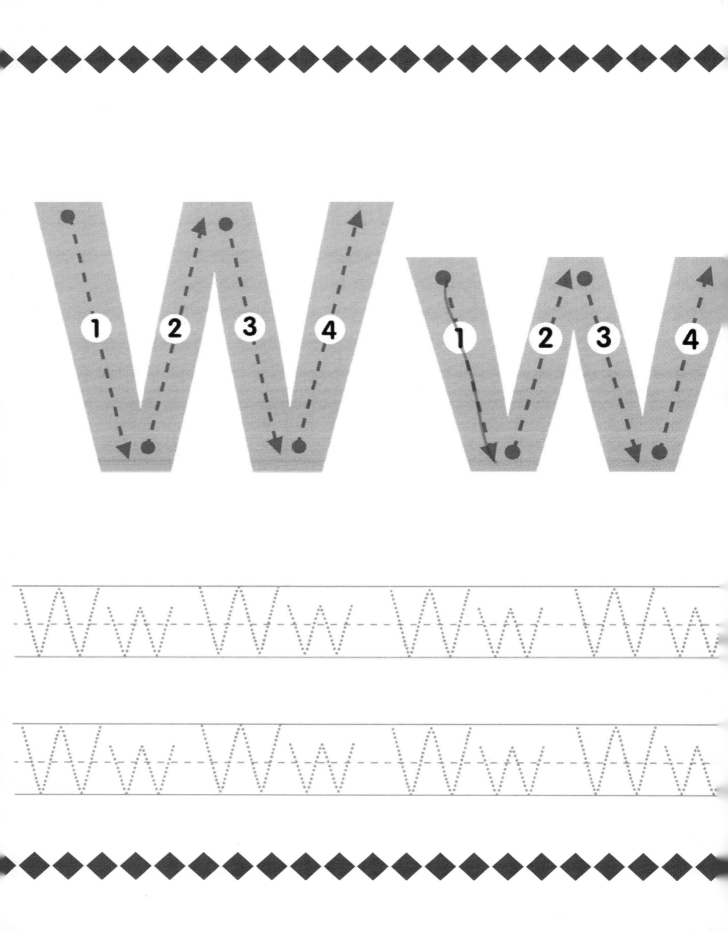

W is for worm

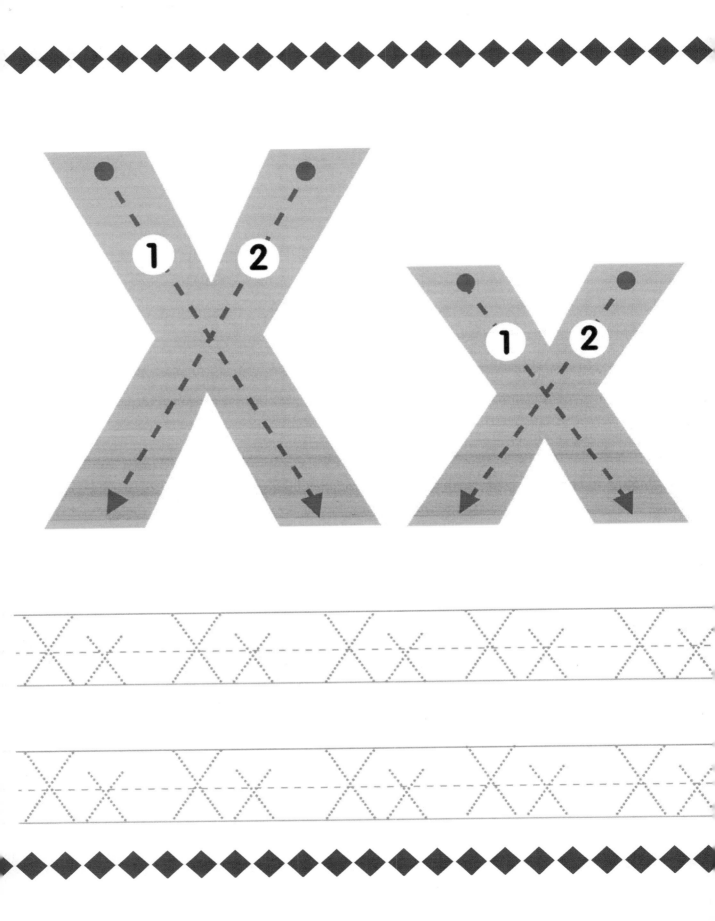

X is for x-ray fish

X X X X X X X X X X X X X

X X X X X X X X X X X X X

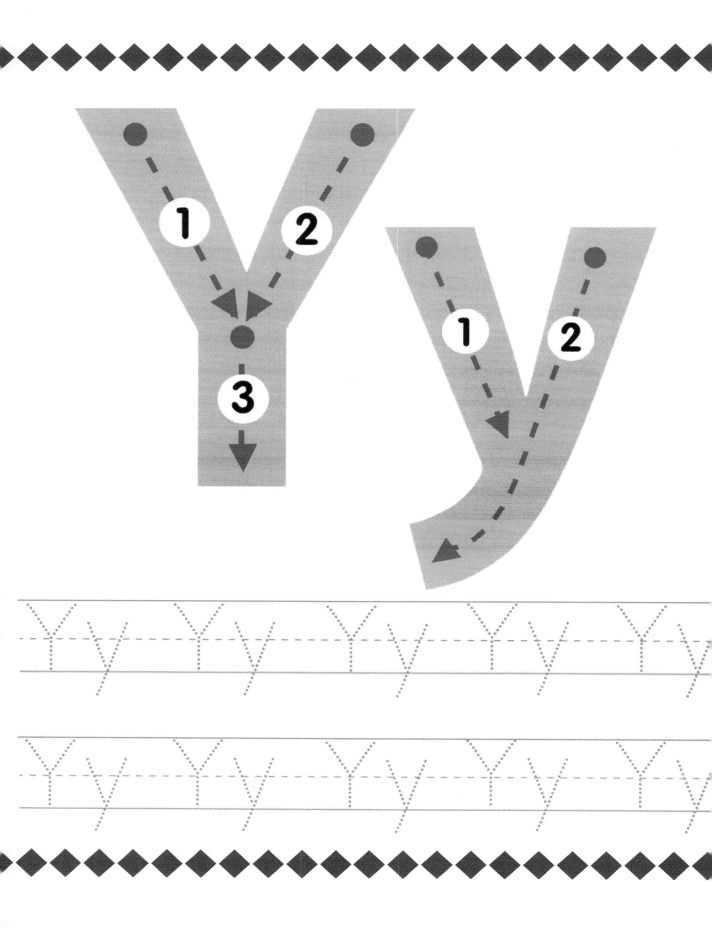

Y is for yak

Y y Y y Y y Y y Y y Y y

Y y Y y Y y Y y Y y Y y

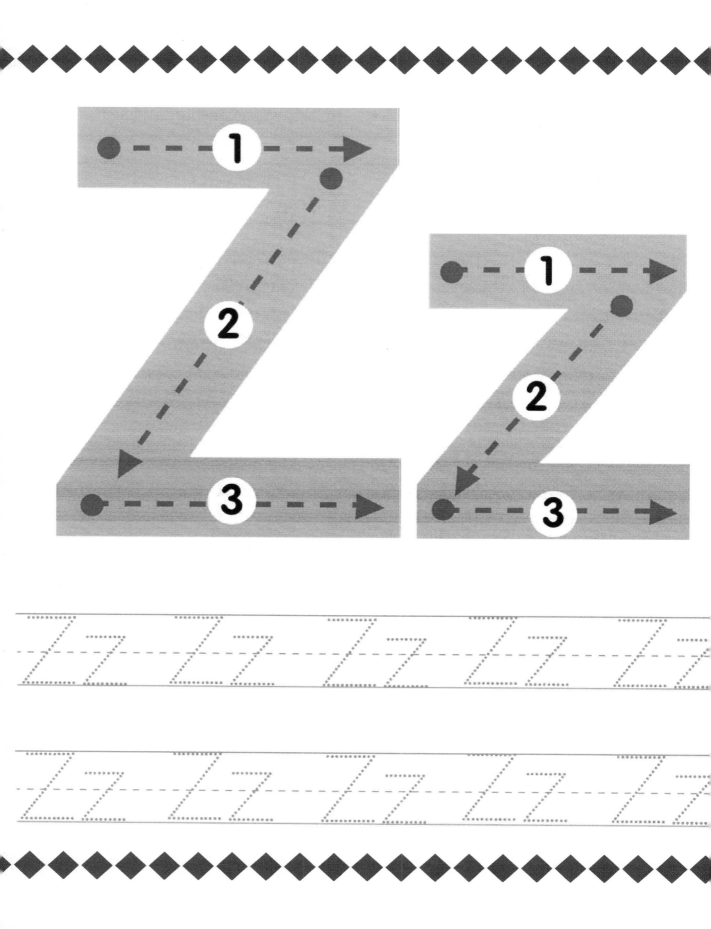

Z is for zebra

57141645R00062

Made in the USA
Middletown, DE
16 December 2017